Glory Holes

Boston Gordon

Harbor Editions
Small Harbor Publishing

Glory Holes
Copyright © 2022 BOSTON GORDON
All rights reserved.

Cover art by James Hoelscher
Cover design by Taylor Blevins
Book layout by Allison Blevins and Hannah Martin

GLORY HOLES
BOSTON GORDON
ISBN 978-1-957248-90-5
Harbor Editions,
an imprint of Small Harbor Publishing

CONTENTS

i. wrecking ball / 9

ii. you are alone in a small blue room / 10

iii. the region of want / 12

iv. adios snowglobe, it was all a dream / 14

v. june / 17

vi. grace / 19

vii. memorial day / 22

vii. abandon / 25

ix. when the world stops / 29

x. years ago / 31

xi. it's not like you're into cuffing season / 34

xii. the body / 37

xiii. the long war / 38

Glory Holes

I. WRECKING BALL

remember boy, the time I pushed
you off the wingdam. kissed you
in the river weeds, fucked up on pints.
cue chalk between our teeth, you pulled
on my armpit hair and I teased
you for losing your glasses.
you didn't want to get in my way.
so you let me alone, but I was always
looking for you behind the after hours club
or between the pines, where we licked
whiskey by the train tracks like lost boys together—
fat with sex and vice. ain't no one get it.
ain't no one know what it's like to feel
your hard on in the warm creek
and smack the smell of your good ideas
off your thighs. I feel your clover tongue.
the way you hock your spit on my ass.
the way you tune me—a handmade fiddle.
the way god is watching us swig,
our faces like we are full. like
your knuckles hit my teeth. the bad boys.
how we are so many fucking rivers?
how I have fallen in love with
your belly button in a bathroom stall?
your shoulders on a pine covered
marsh, you let me suck you off,
as long as I checked you for ticks after.

II. YOU ARE ALONE IN A SMALL BLUE ROOM

The blue light from the bridge licks your toes.
The blue rug is blue because you messed it with pen ink
or blue paint from the protest, depending
on who you meant to be that day.
It can be blue to be you because you love
the color of it. You know the color
when you first kiss someone you are scared
of, and they say they know who you are.
Scared because you saw them in a dream,
and in the dream, they held a piece of charcoal,
blue and dusty, to your forehead and said
you are the son of god. That was before
you knew the prayers they told themself.
In the dream, you felt them muttering
like a blue bird on a Carolina fencepost,
words that only make sense to the mouth
they belong to. When you kissed,
you remembered the prayers and also
the dream. They held you behind a statue
like you were the crown jewel, the trophy
for a lifetime of suffering. Someone who knew
what it was to be kept from jumping off the bridge.
You wore blue that night because you like it. They
had blue eyes like a movie star and a blue bicycle laid
by the river. You wanted the river to be blue too,
but it was only blue because of the lights
from the hospital and the easy wake of canoes.
You touched the blue artery in their neck
and reminded them they were alive.
Years later their blue bike got bent
by a yellow station wagon

and you screamed *blue!* and ran to clutch
their artery. You took them to the blue hospital,
waited to see how bruised their body was.
You held them, talked about the dream,
and they tried to tell you not to dream so much—
it's bad for your blues—but you insisted
in the dream blue bubbles and a purple sky
and you could see everything—the prayers,
the bridge, the bicycle—and you
were against blue brick in a blue alleyway
singing I know who you are too.

III. THE REGION OF WANT
After D.A. Powell

A summer spent staring into a graveyard
with boys who had feet smaller than mine
and couldn't whistle worth a damn. *Damn.*

It was hot like falling asleep behind the field and staring
into the faded lines of aged headstones. Just
a toothpick behind my ear and grass stains on my ass.

Years away from the summers I dreamed of
in boyhood, a whistle, there you are boy, leaning
against a headstone in the graveyard

of the city, hot along the water, hot
even though the nights are still a little shorter.

I'd grown shorter through the winter,
but somehow here was a bottle of rainwater
for a birthday I didn't know about. Mostly,

I thought about your feet
which was all I could stand to look
at through the smoke.

I am half a spliff though when you fall
at my feet and call me boy. It's all on my fingertips—
you, freshwater, and the splinters of old wild roses.

If I am half a spliff, smoke me and listen:
Two boys stand on their shoe tips, thighs shaking.
Look, it's the bad alleyway with the bathhouse.

Steam and men slink through the door cracks, hot.
But look here, back to the boys. This one
has eyes like gunfire and unchains a bike

from a parking meter with fine-tuned knuckles.
They depart, and the alleyway seems to split
like a pitted peach or more grey and broken

like a knocked over headstone. Look up.
The other boy walks due north, nose in the air
like a beagle. Stops to roll a joint

in the trolley car cemetery where the old monsters
seem to hum in their rotting and are full
of explosive vines of wild rose, poison oak.

The death of a train car is slow. A match strike.
Both boys again. This one looks waterlogged
and stoned, with heavy tits. That one is breathy.

Says, *Come back. Take up my space. Everyone
is leaving.* The other is howling, maybe.

IV. ADIOS SNOWGLOBE, IT WAS ALL A DREAM

It was hot, and we had paper cuts all over our fingers
in the shapes of the initials of everyone we'd ever

known except they weren't paper cuts they were glass
slices and there were still little pieces

in the grooves of my palms that I couldn't pry out
it wasn't everyone's initials but everyone's

belly buttons and breasts all scarred up
in hospital gowns after a whole row of surgeries

you said *drink the wine*
I said *yes please* and let some drip into my glass shards

outside there was an elderly toad
who kept watch over us

sprung up and down the unpaved drive
gulped nice oxygen through his toad skin

made sure no bad men made it to the house without
squashing him and turning back in toad murder guilt

everyone's scars faded
even my own glass scars and we felt good

you said it was a terrible thing to dream about dead end
jobs I said it was more terrible to work them

I hardly believed myself
I still don't believe myself

so instead you got two paper bags and two cans of beer
and you took me to an oak tree that didn't look

like an oak tree split in half and growing back together
almost a graft more like a glass wound

we ate peaches out of an oak tree
I don't know how we made that trick happen

but we did I told you about my deepest regrets
that I hadn't kissed you first

that I'd taken the lazy job that fired me anyway
that once I didn't read anything for six months

you told me how afraid you were of little pills
of my panic attacks of your father of being brave

it was almost night by then
and it was all you could do to hold me

like a silver spoon
so I let you

the air conditioner rattled and I had bad dreams
of all the bad things that had ever happened to me

and my glass cuts grew swollen in the humidity
and you purred like a tiger lamb while you slept

after dark I could hear cicadas grandfather toad
the turning of my wine stomach

I was afraid but you felt strong you had no hair
you had eyelids big as the Arizona desert

I let myself forget the dreams
where I finally jump out the window

the way I ruined my fingers the time
my dog died so my dad put a gun to his head

I remembered why I was there in the first place
I remembered why you were there at all

I felt good I felt bad too
You love misery you always joked

I love misery I can't help it

V. JUNE

It's June, impossible again.
That trochaic phrase
foxtrots through my head.

I'm in love with myself.
That's why I drink too much.
Tawny beers disappear

in spilled stains on my tank top.
I'm in love with myself.
So who shouldn't fuck me? Take me

home, take me out back and shoot me.
Who the fuck cares really? Some nights
I stare like everyone is a pebble to suck on,

a salt block to lick,
a hand to bite in early June.
If my hand brushes my zipper,

will that man over there
want to fuck me in the ass?
Will those two ask me

to go home with them?
If they do, will I remember where I am?
I am that weed lurking in the garden—

stylish, stout, and easily pulled at.
It's June. Shouldn't I be better at this?
Yank on me, and I won't remember.

I'll wake up with a hangover,
and blood on my sheets,
wishing I was more in love with myself.

VI. GRACE

I learned how to take
my body and make bad noises.
I quit smoking, I quit drinking,
I quit sugar and coffee.

Then I smoked again,
and then I drank again,
and then I fell down the waterfall again,
and again and again.

There is lightning on the top
of the mountain. I am scared
of lightning, so I jump down the waterfall
and have a panic attack anyway.

I used to write in the graveyard
and now I sit in the church
and vacillate between *god did this to me* or
each day I don't jump is a grace given.

I don't know how
to tell anyone this.
Is it immoral to punch someone
who has punched you first?

Is it immoral to spread
one's body the way that I do?
I guess it's not grace when you get head
behind a dumpster.

The scratch marks on my hip
feel more like staying on top

of the mountain, than licking
the salt at the bottom of the fall.

So trauma betrays me again. Forget
what happened to my body
by sewing myself up
like making an orchard out of twigs.

I'm weaving again, and again
I am flaming. I am alive
when someone touches me like I'm
their favorite pair of blue jeans.

I'm chasing that through the churchyard.
I'm singing about it on Sunday mornings.
I've lost it again.
I don't know how to do this.

Let me try to tell you like this.
Someone did a bad thing to my body,
and then I grew up.
More people, more bad, more body.

Then I tried to jump out of the window.
More people, more body, something else.
Then the window started following me around,
and I got faster than the window.

Then the window swallowed me whole,
so I sucked on more bodies and cut
my finger on more zippers.

I became the champion of late nights
and early mornings. I listened to pirate radio
because I love a life full of static,
and low stakes danger.

I liked the way boys held coke cans.
I liked the way barbecue sauce tasted.
I liked it when you'd call me horrible things
to make me hard up.

It's said that some things
only strike twice. But here I am
living in the forever
of my own wounds.

There was a man once
who would regularly sneak up behind me
when I was dancing and lick my neck.
It was offensive but beautiful.

In that moment, I could think
of nothing but the stranger's
gruesome tongue on my skin:
the invasion of it, the way I'd get hard.

I worry you can't help a person
who feels things like that.

VII. MEMORIAL DAY

you count on boy
who leaves tooth marks
on tall cans of beer

your friends spend the night
jumping off the roof
to see who can live longest

cigarettes whistle
behind your diving body
like impromptu firecrackers

by morning you've forgotten
how to read
how to spit in public

you laugh
order grease trap
take out

you read sappy poems
to good friends
collect old band-aids

you climb scaffolding
tag windows with
cartoon birds

wheat-paste over
your own desire
run back to find tooth

marks wait at the bar
get pinned against the wall
slosh your bitter ale on t-shirt

boy hugs you against
broad frame of body
you hear their tongue

click against their teeth
like getting bitten
cologne like muddled mint

lips sticky from summer
could drop
to knees & lick

the sweat from their calves
did they gnaw on it
to protect you

you think
you'll split
in two

have to trace
the shapes of old
hitching posts

on a walk to
poetry reading
like you can tether

yourself or be rescued
by a set of platform pumps
too big for your flat feet

cotton-polyester socks
stuck to the insides
you're falling over

so you can be
sticky with wanting
the boy to look at you

flash lipstick mouth
in your direction

VIII. ABANDON

Every day is the last day
of summer you hustle
to the river you bike
to the cemetery you should never
have hung around cemeteries
with girls who are like ghosts

ghosting you after she put
a dick on for you
cupped your face
while she did you real
dirty made you think love was
something for her too

everyone is wearing cotton
at this poetry reading it's *very*
last day of summer of them
you're drinking bad beer
like your style
is waiting in a barbershop

like your style is thinking
about a guy you might blow later
if he wants to come
if he'll make it worth your while
sex work is barely
asking for what you need

it's not impressive to her
that you can crack eggs
with one hand she will never
really eat your honey

bees make honey inside of bellies
spit it up for you to eat like a violation

your feelings get very hurt
she socks you in your guts
red wine comes out and stains
your white v-neck like a birthmark
your belly bled through
you might survive this abandonment too

this abandonment
like a rusted can you swallowed
whole, you carry a knife
in case you meet yourself
down an alleyway and need
to slit the throat of your own sorrow

karma is a drowned goose
are you venomous
or poisonous
what feeds the river
mouth of *abandonment*
ouch, that word hurts

bartender from the club
pays you twenty dollars
to beat your ass with a pleather club
fucks you after closing time
he barely likes looking
at you

you work twelve hour gig work
they don't pay you
they won't let you leave
negotiations go nowhere
they don't believe in sick days

you bounce

you'd rather spend
your summer of unemployment
of abandon, on booze
you figure you could use more
lunch break fucks before
back to work

at the leather bar
you meet an Alabama man
who's not *gay* just really likes
how gay guys suck cock
you're disappointed
giving head is not your gift

you jerk him off on a ride
to his hotel, don't get
his name won't tell you
his job he's hiding
something you figure
must be a wife

he orders you a car
shuts the door
elevator is busted so you run
twelve flights of fire stairs
to catch your ride and pray
you're not abandoned

losing your job
the worst break up
you know why someone
grew tired fucking you
why'd your job get tired
of exploiting you

you wore a good suit
you owned two of them
you most flexible team player
guess it wasn't prudent
to party all night
chasing bartender ass

like you didn't have a job
like you didn't know you'd
lose your job
swallow the pink slip
they won't keep jerking
you off

it is summer of abandon
thank you for your interest in
thank you for your interest in
your email box of shame
joblessness a teetotaler's hangover
what you thought you had abandoned

you a dog on the side of road
your friend who abandoned you
would definitely not
drive by the dog not great
to use dog metaphors
abandon that real quick

you've done it now
what do people want from you
to see your ass your collar
you float downstream
tail tucked between legs abandoned
thank you for your interest

IX. WHEN THE WORLD STOPS

you jerk off, you suck
your own nipple, you lick
the computer screen
hoping to taste
the cumshot

you stick a bottle up your ass
choke on the dregs of your beer
hump the arm of the couch
hope that gets you off
in time to jump off the roof

you suspect you are
the center of the world
you feel so ugly, you tape
your tits in different positions
making your chest more grotesque

tape starts to tear your skin
you scrub the wound
like some furious spring
cleaning (is there anything clean
about the spring anymore?)

who will want to eat you
alive or dead or modified
no one is eating anymore
no one is gloryholing anymore
nothing glorious left for you

you pervert
on the hot roof

you worrier
of what makes
one unclean

no grace if
you can't compare
a back alley blowjob
to a cry in the church pew
you don't have either anymore

the world stops
you watch *Dawson's Creek*
think about which of your sex
partners is most like Pacey
(it's you, of course, you glib hottie)

you catalogue your free porn
by the length it takes
for you to climax
you stare at your library books
like they're contaminated

we aren't in this together
you get your pants off
you wag your ass
what the fuck else
are you supposed to do?

X. YEARS AGO

Years ago
I got hard
thinking
about yr
neck. Here

in the car
half faded
I want
to jerk off
but the company
is plentiful.

We are driving
to the leather
bar by the beach
and we get
free drinks
at the hotel
to get us red.

We have boys
to entertain.
My shorts
are barely
and I'm ready
to make you
hard.

Drag friend
squeezes
my shoulder

and warns me
that I have a good
life and you
are not in it
and not worth it.

Dear man
uniformed
for the business
of rubbing his dick
on patrons' shoes
licks the underside
of my boot
and declares it
adorable.

In that
deliciousness
I learned
what it was
to lament
to want
to tongue
yr geode
like ancient ways
to find salt
in the hills.

I could
have fucked
the hole
in the wall
but instead
we left
we got sodas
at Taco Bell

and I described
your eyebrows
thinking
that would cool
me off.

XI. IT'S NOT LIKE YOU'RE INTO CUFFING SEASON

you're an amphibian in heat
the sun comes out
you fall in love
you kiss her and your glasses
knock together until you
find the right rhythm
and you don't mind
a long walk home
with nose prints
blurring your lenses

wiped out on the deck
letting yourself get dehydrated
flesh heavy and sun-pink
you fall in love
with your knees
you like the desperate
aerobics of dropping
to the floor
you love bruises
you love the girl in canada
who bit your shoulder
so hard you didn't notice
you like being stoned
you like the pocket
inside your vest
that holds a tallboy
beer like a cradle
like something you
made yourself
labor of loving

all the birds in this town
are so fucking horny
puffed up pigeons
show off your arms
throw a punch
at the puffed up man who kicked
you out of the backroom
gentlemen only
you get high in the park instead
conspicuous and teenaged
even though it's legal here
you like indiscretions
like boning in the woods
or smelling like cum
when you go through the tsa line

a date bails last minute
you feel a little mangled
by this crushing
summertime is only
small sadnesses
that you stroke lovingly
when you could just get over them
it's not like you're into cuffing season
you're an animal of the swamp
coming out of the wet
holes of late may
fueled by instinct
learned in close calls

you live in the loamlands
you lick your own bicep
clammy from sunburn
and sex and salt
it tastes like last summer
you kissed someone under

the juniper trees out west
rode your bike across the river
sang about her beautiful porch
stood up while you pedaled
like when you were a scrawny kid
biking to the creek for a swim
oblivious to that year's drought
dangerous blunder
for amphibians to make

XII. THE BODY

There is, of course, the cutting of the body.
Lean away from that for a minute. Stand
in the middle of a shack on fabric row
and browse the cardboard bricks wrapped
in lace and taffeta. You can feel the taffeta
like the bustle skirt thrown at you from stage
at the burlesque show. Where you sweat
under orange show lights and notice the ordinary
nature of breasts, watch the sequins swept aside.
The breasts are bags of wine. Your breasts
are hanging hunks that you often relate to cuttings.
Because people you know sometimes cut theirs
off so as not to look like you. You are a bust
and ass and legs that make a man say, *Ahem.
Miss, what're you trying to tell me with those legs?*
You're shocked because your boyfriend fucks
you like a real man, but everyone is looking
at your hormonal fat, your body like a melting
sculpture. So you tie your shoes or lock your bike
and look down and think about the cutting.
Think that even in another body, even after
that barter with the mud wasp and surgeon,
you would still not be settled. Not just this
body, but all body. So in the fabric store
the shears make that good sound like rubbing
two nickels together and you're back
to the six yards of burlap unfolding
on the countertop and the body steps away
from cut. Cut. It refuses to be just a body.

XIII. THE LONG WAR

it's winter or
it's the last day of winter
and they're calling for a second war

it's winter
it's the second day of the new decade
they're calling

you have only just accepted
what happened to your father's father
who died long before you were born

left the men you are made from
to cry into bottles of Boone's Farm
their hands blue and holding little white bones

you imagine a world where your father
wasn't your father, was the man he wanted
to be which was the man his father was

even drunker, and mean
but for good reason, the war hard etched
he could smell the blood from men's scalps

it's winter or the last day of winter
and you have been hurting yourself
because you are just a scared little boy

you are hurting yourself because you are you
boys in gym class spit in between swipes
with their hockey sticks

spit lands on your shinbone and that feeling
will stay with you for the rest of your life
the hot of a man's insides spilled onto you

the spitting boys talk about the war
salivate over the day they'll enlist
how many men they'll kill with their trigger fingers

how many women will want to blow them
and you figure you could join the army
but you remember how you are

how the sight of your own skinned knee
makes you dizzy, makes you wretch
from the smell of warm blood

you're in junior high and these boys
won't join the war because in five years they'll
be dead or college bound

there is no in between
it's the second day of the new decade
and the war has carried on for two thirds of your life

it's been so constant you barely think
about it anymore, you don't flinch
don't know the hundreds of thousands of bodies

instead you get stoned and watch a documentary
about the Vietnam war and cry to a Simon and
Garfunkel song like it explains how war happens

like you didn't see it happen
like it wasn't happening since the year
you were born, but came out barely alive
it's the new decade and you remember

protesting the war, you remember actions taken
now you're preoccupied with bodies

you exchange nudes on scruff
you jerk off and talk to this military guy
who's on the DL and looking for some hole

he asks you what you're into
are you into this? this? how about this?
he says you seem like just what he's *hunting for*

you remember the boys again, spitting on you
how they'd wait until the end of the day
when you'd crossed the parking lot

they'd adjust their american flag baseball hats
and spit on their hands and seize you
hold you down on the ground and choke you

the warmth of their breath terrifying
but kind of a turn on as they pushed your collarbone
harder the macadam scraping your elbows

it was the last days of winter
and boys dreamt of becoming killers
and you dreamt they might kill you

you don't like the the word *hunting*
from the mouth of a man who owns
a us army supplied rifle

so you block him
hope he doesn't sell your nudes
roll your underwear back up
your grandfather killed people in a different century
on a different continent, in a different climate

he smelled the blood until he died

he died and left behind boys who couldn't
feel things anymore, he died
and could not have anticipated you

you belly down on the floor
turned on thinking about spit
but stopped to imagine

it's winter and you stop
consider the warm bodies far away spitting
in the dirt of another continent, too afraid not to

ACKNOWLEDGMENTS

Grateful acknowledgment is made to the editors of the following journals in which these works, or earlier versions of them, first appeared:

American Poetry Review: "the long war"

Bedfellows Magazine: "june"

Guernica: "the body"

PRISM International: "you are alone in a small blue room"

The Fem Magazine: "the region of want

The Tiny: "memorial day bbq"

Tinderbox Magazine: "wrecking ball" and "adios snowglobe"

Stonefruit Magazine: "grace"

Thank you to queer spaces for giving me freedom to desire. Thank you to Shari Caplan, Heather Hughes, and July Westhale for feedback on many of these poems. Thank you to Emory Marino for steadfast support and numinous love. Thank you to James Hoelscher for letting me come back and take up their space.

Boston Gordon (they/he) is a poet from Philadelphia, Pennsylvania. They run the You Can't Kill A Poet reading series—which highlights queer and trans identified writers in Philadelphia. Boston earned their MFA in Poetry through Lesley University. They have previously been published in such places as *PRISM International, Guernica*, and *American Poetry Review*.

www.ingramcontent.com/pod-product-compliance
Lightning Source LLC
Chambersburg PA
CBHW051704040426
42446CB00009B/1304